SaymenSayz

Picture book of Illustrations
VOL. I

Ghostly whale
Jellyfish
Seahorse
Manta ray
Octopus
Water world
Turtle
Fish couple
Lamp fish
Bubble fish

10 original illustrations of water animals

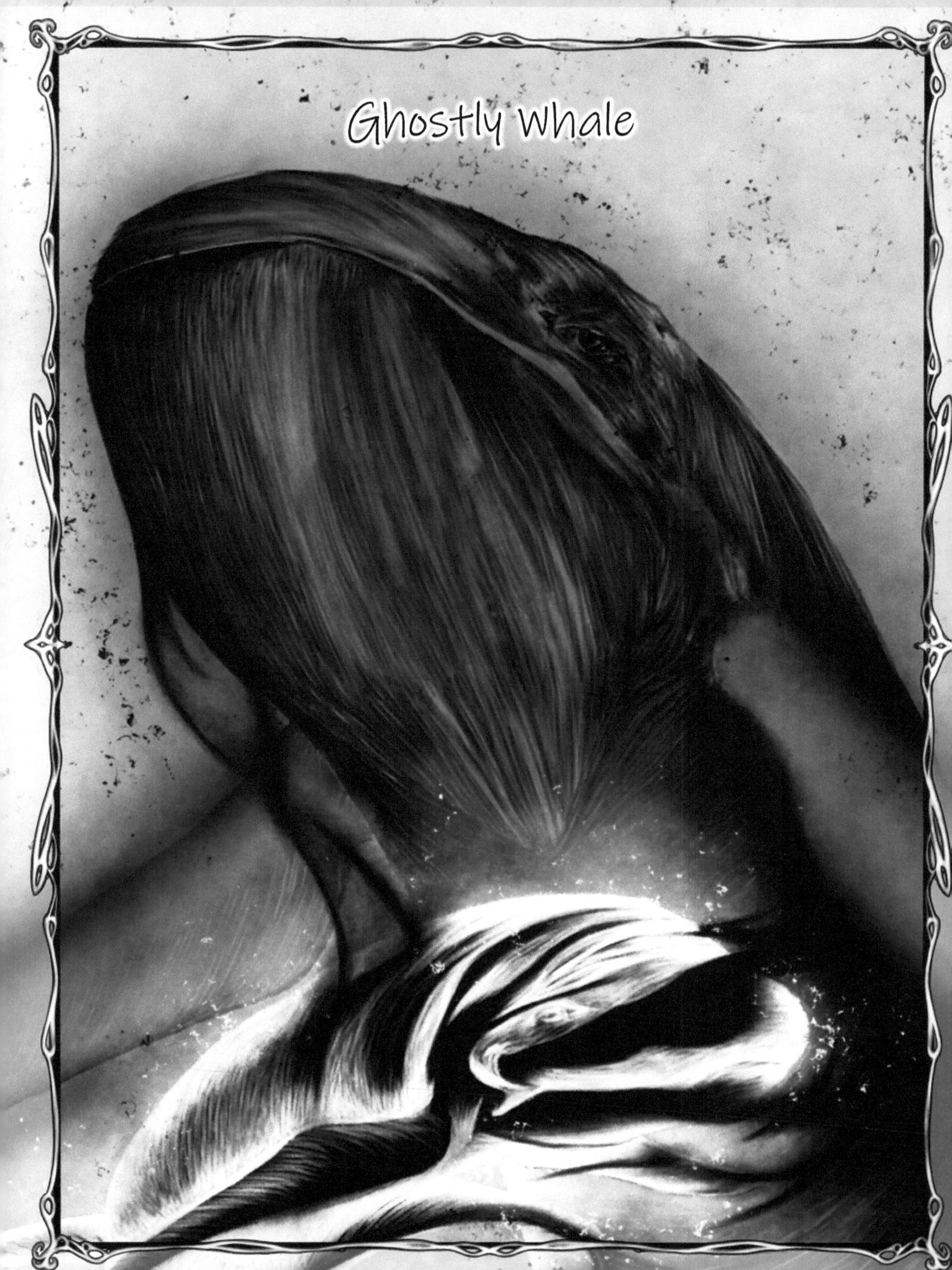
Ghostly whale

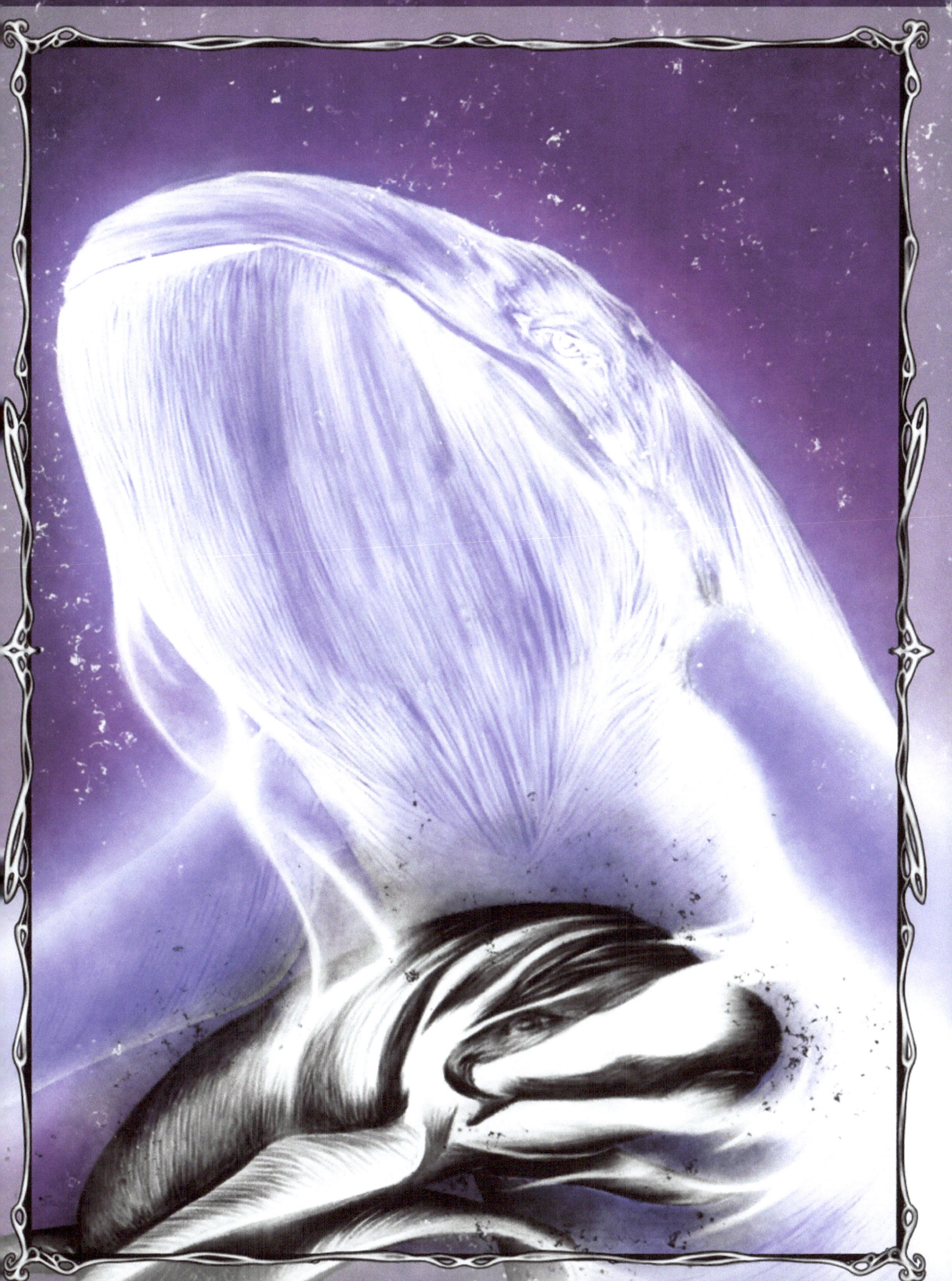

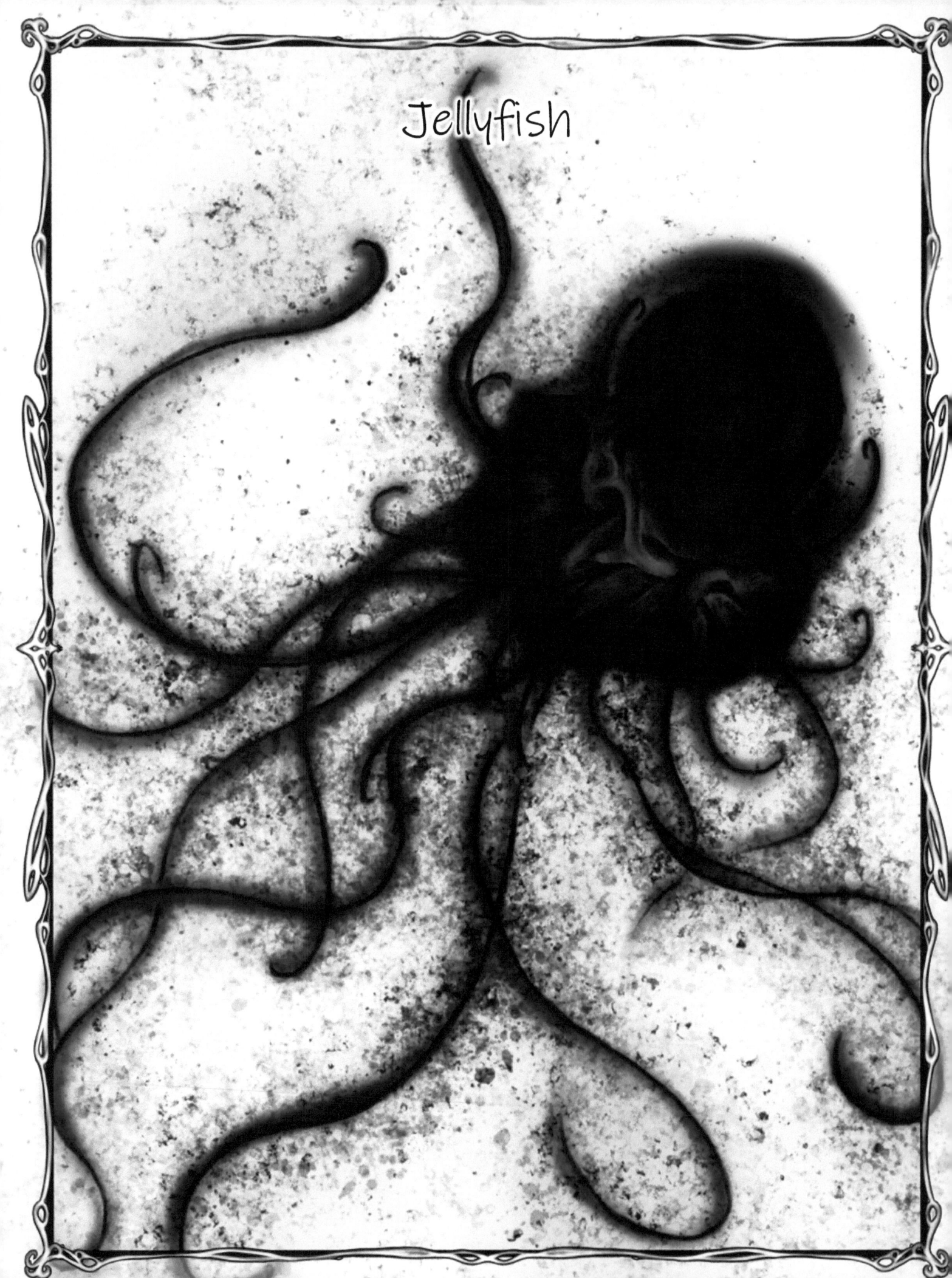

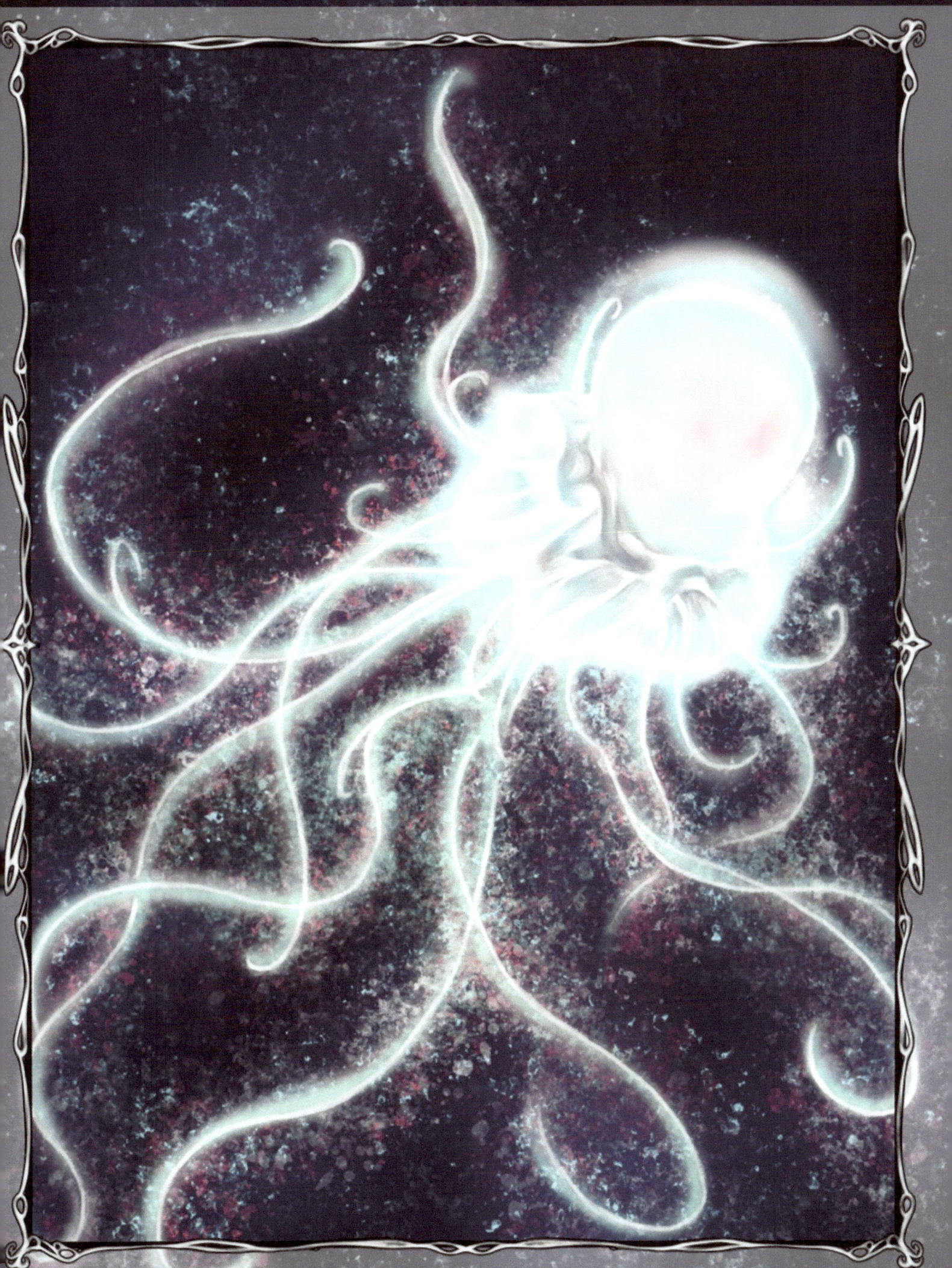

Seahorse

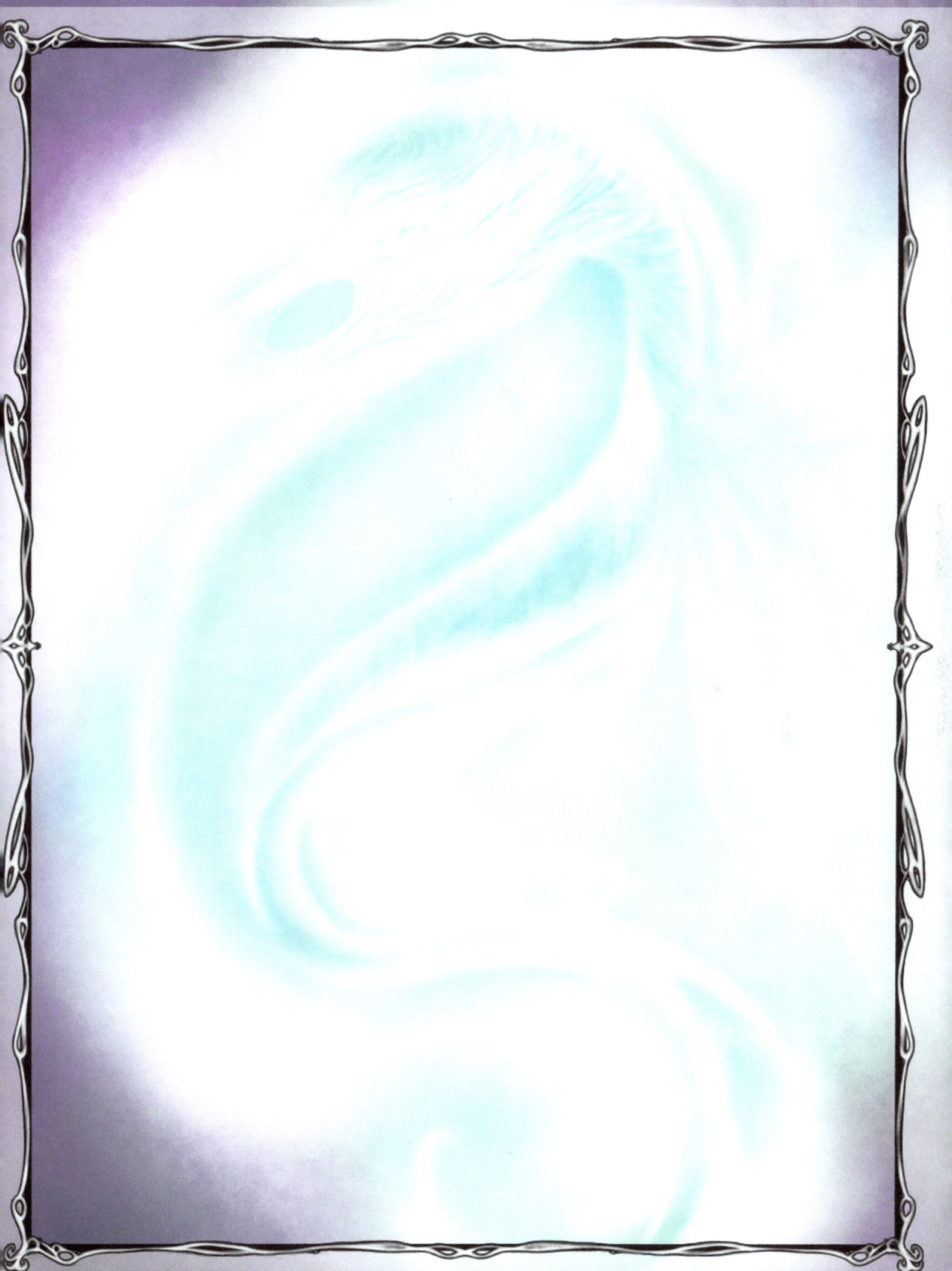

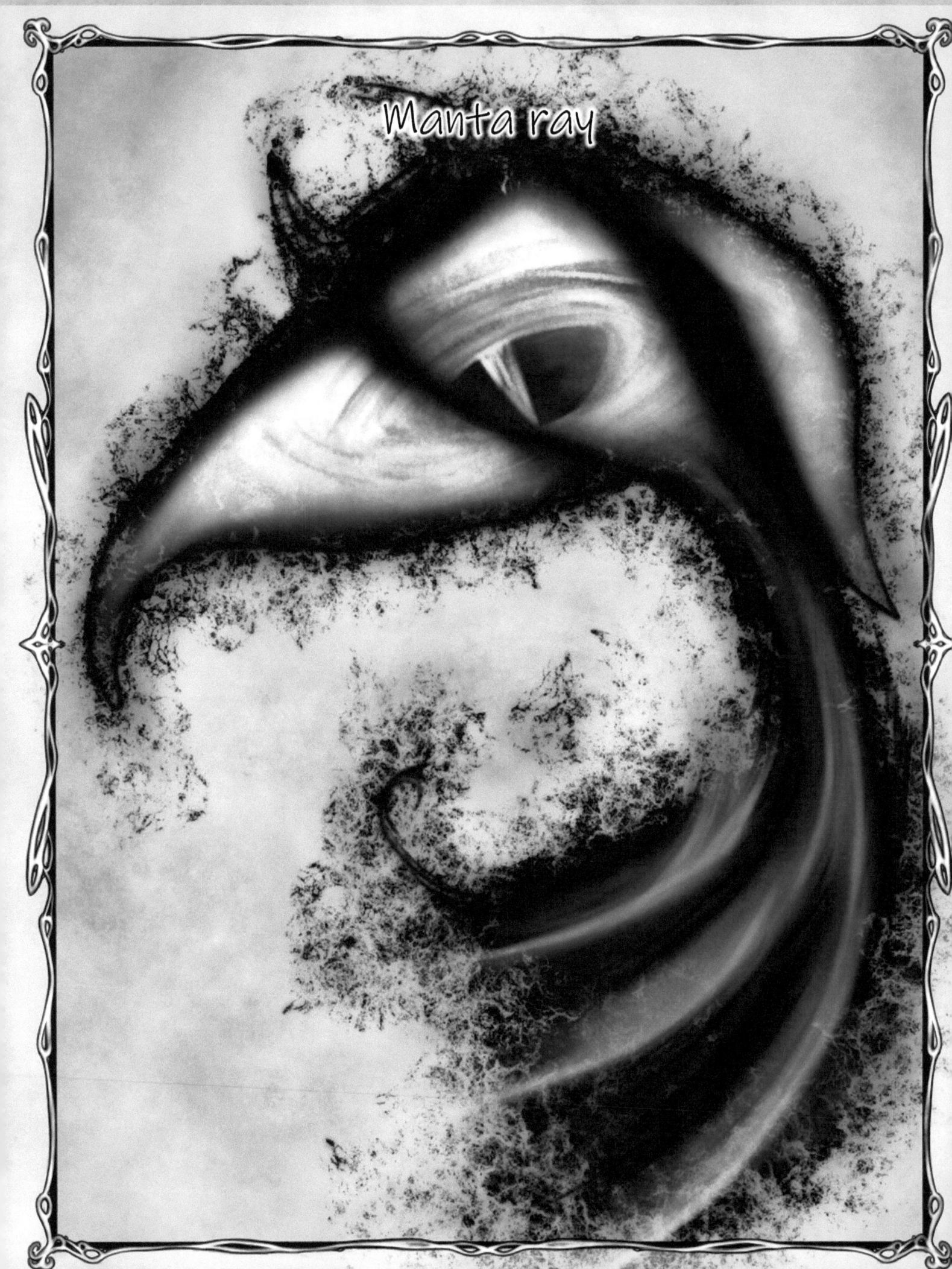

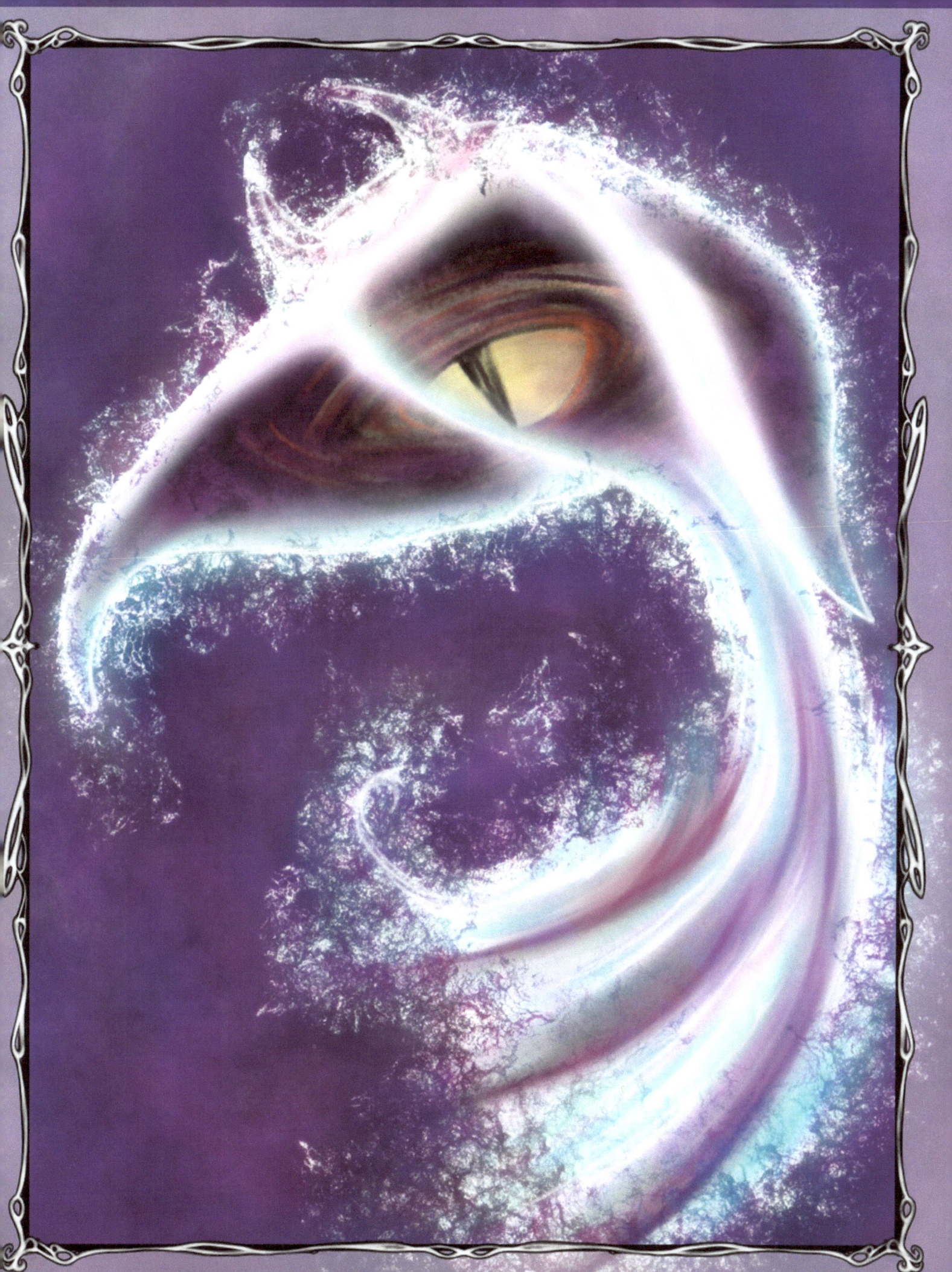

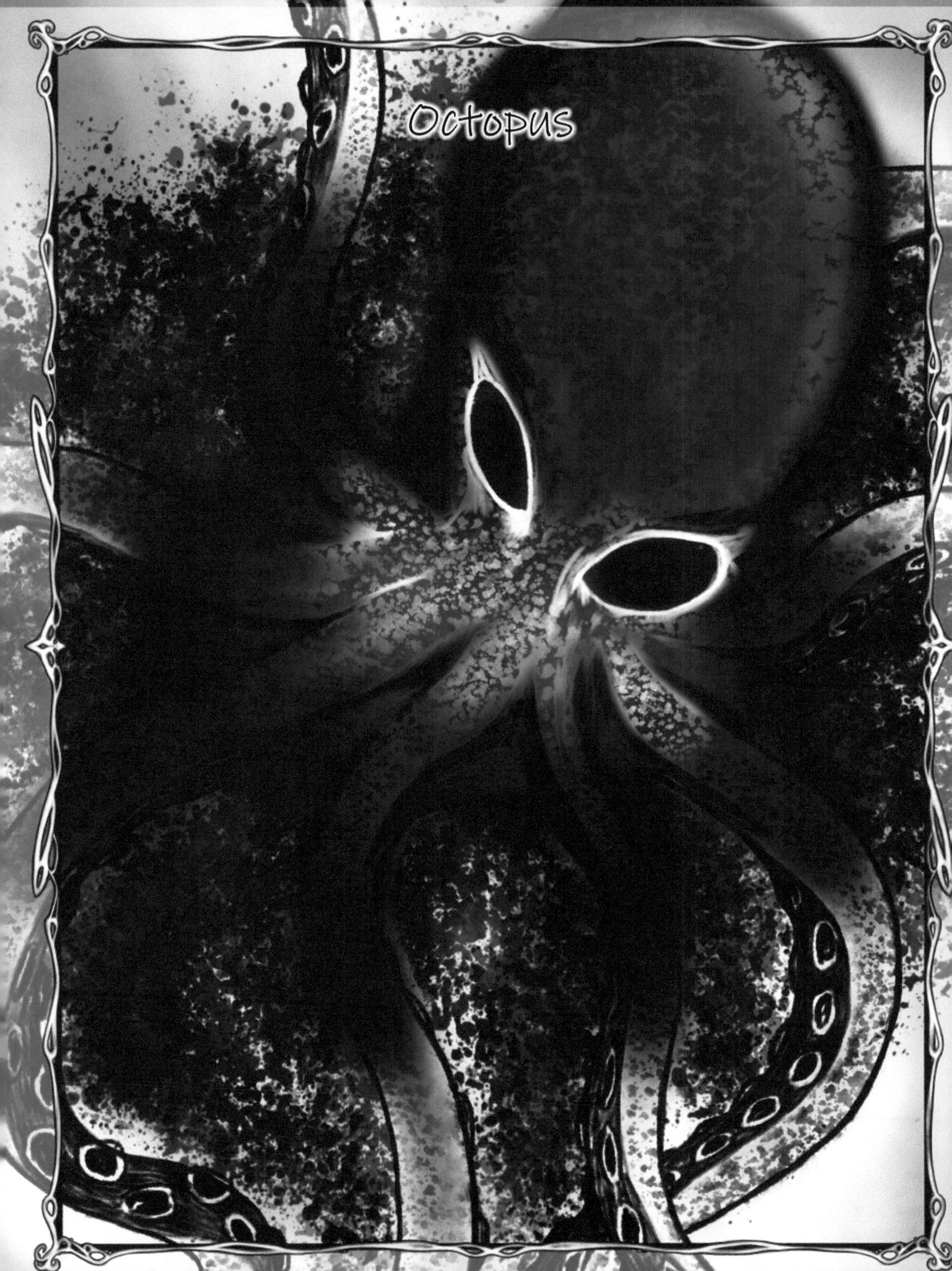

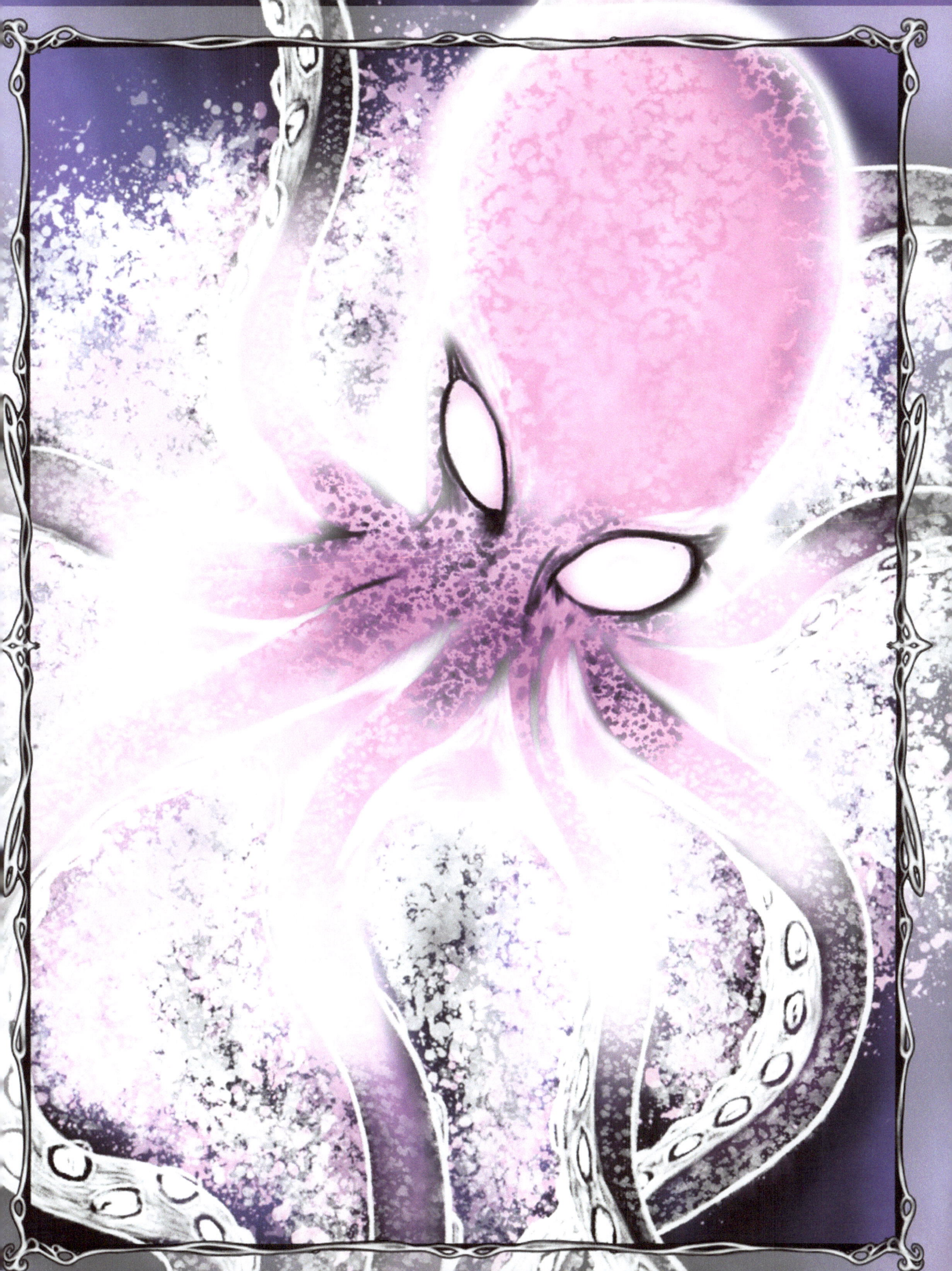

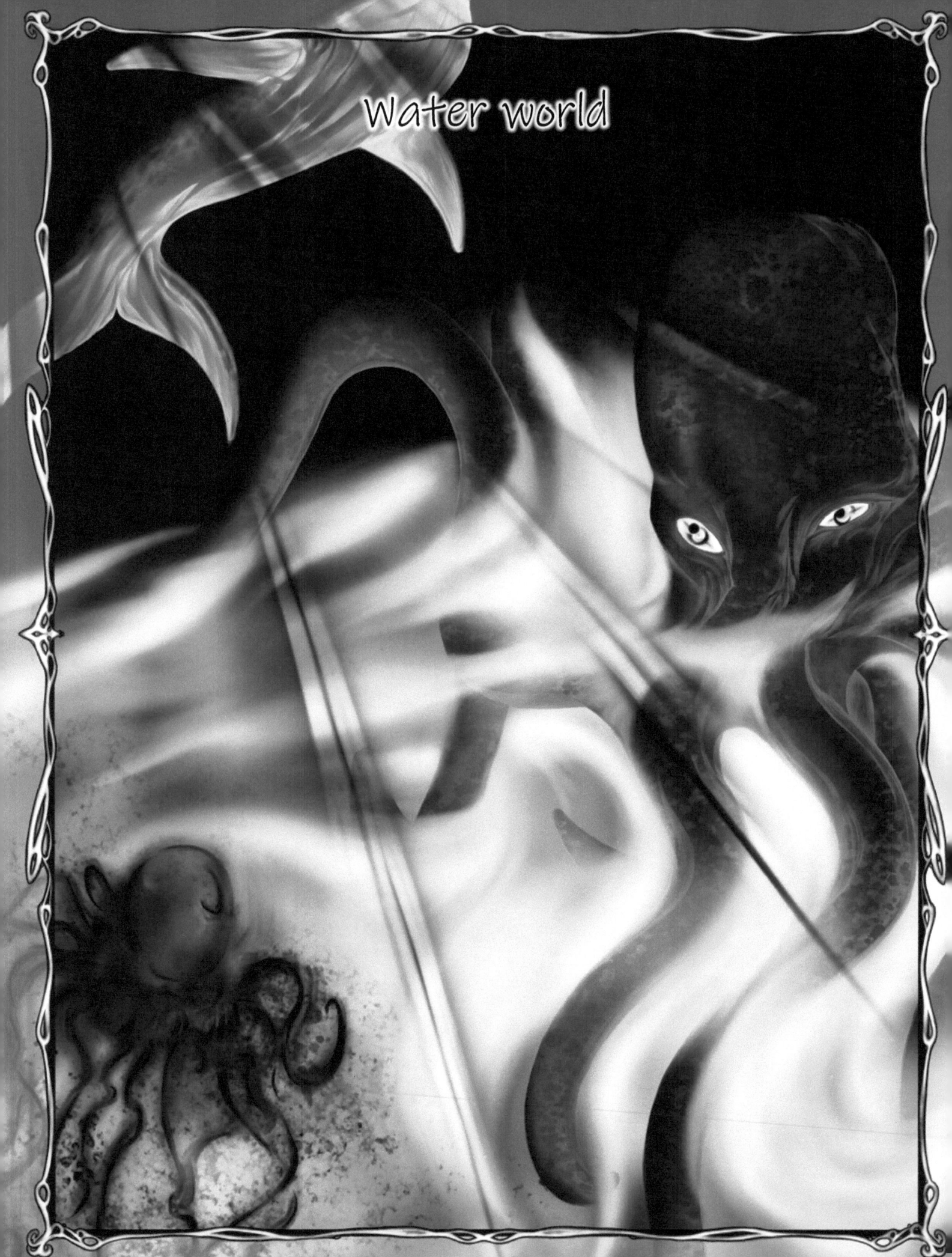

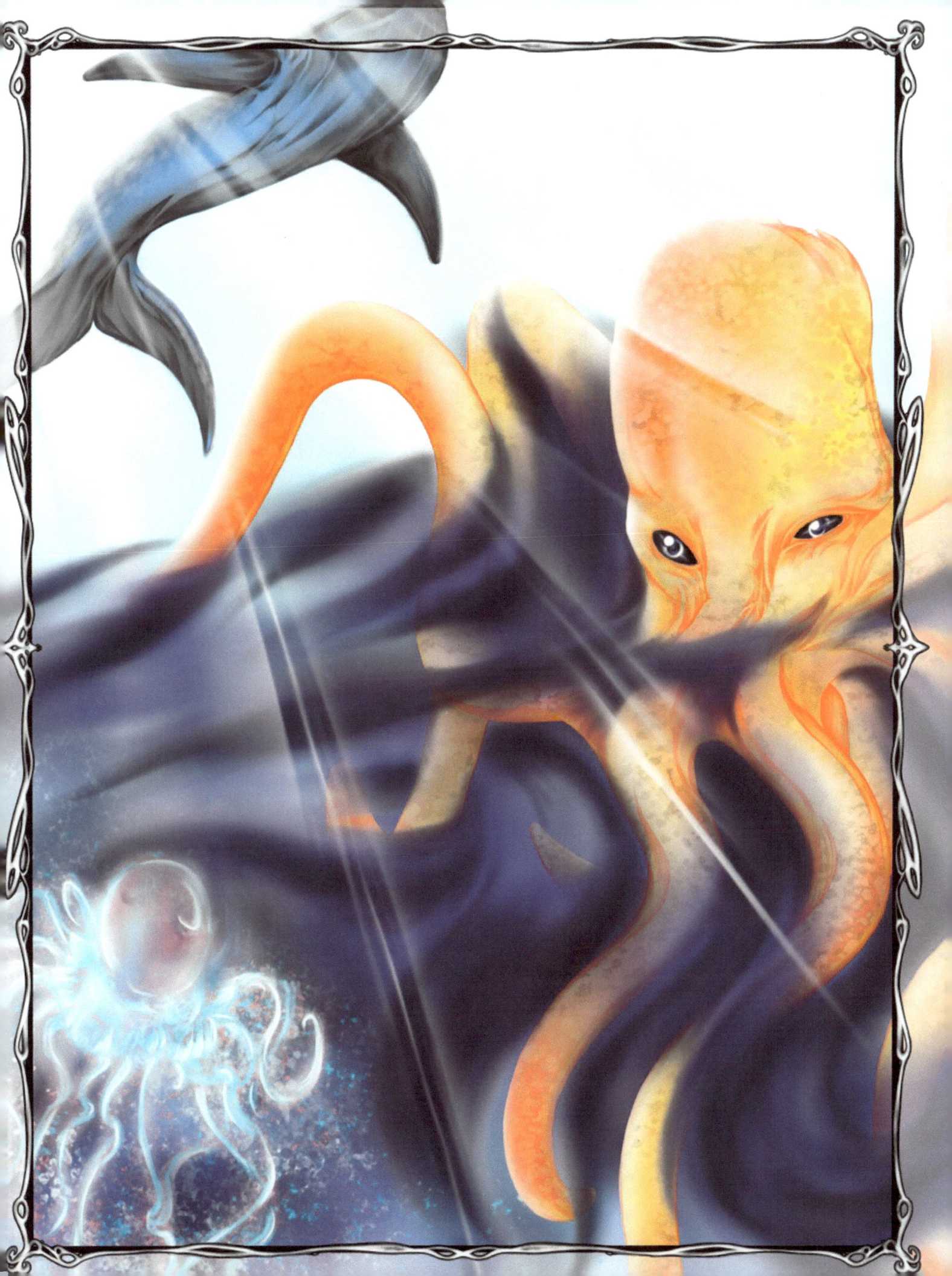

Turtle

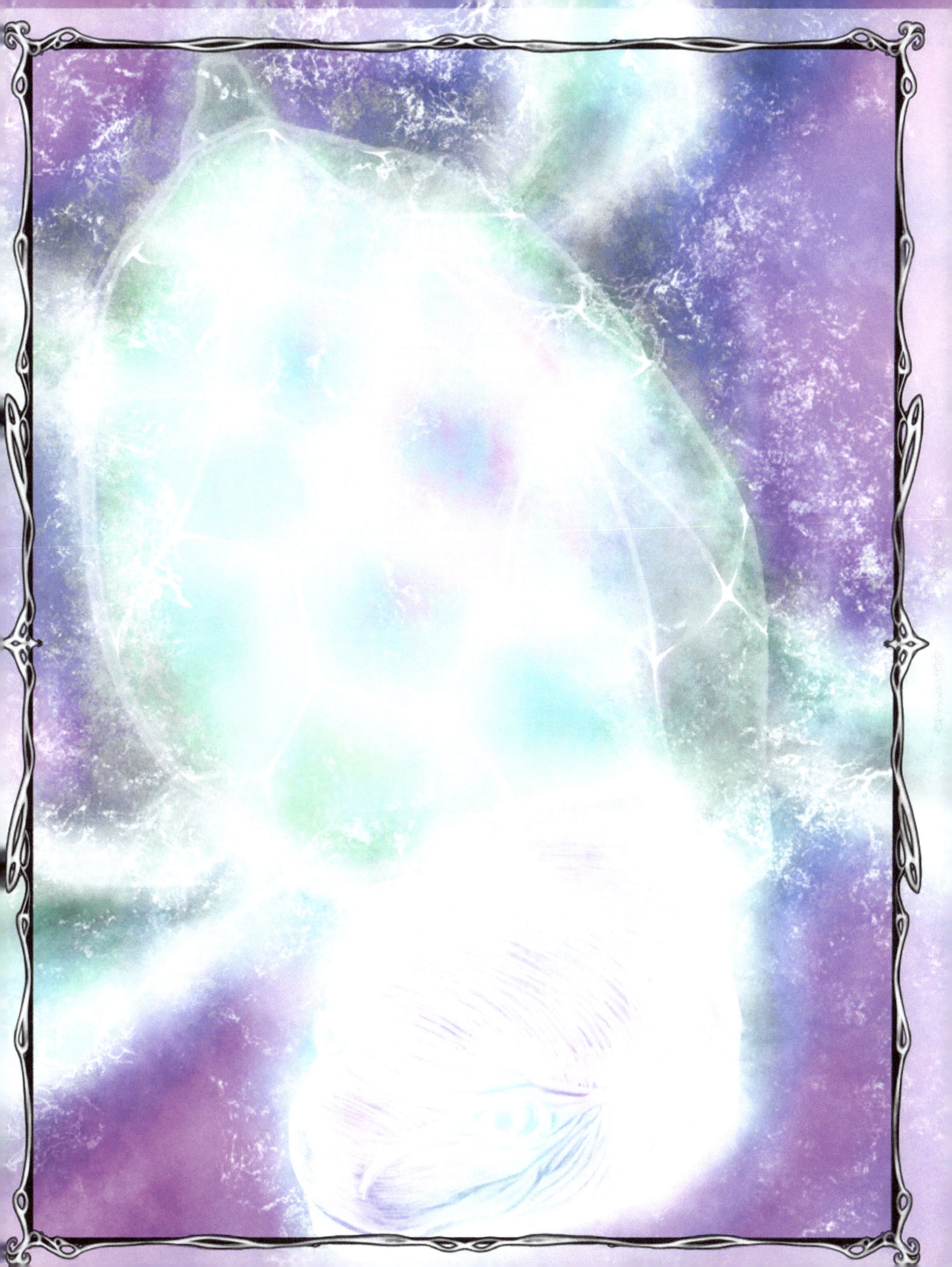

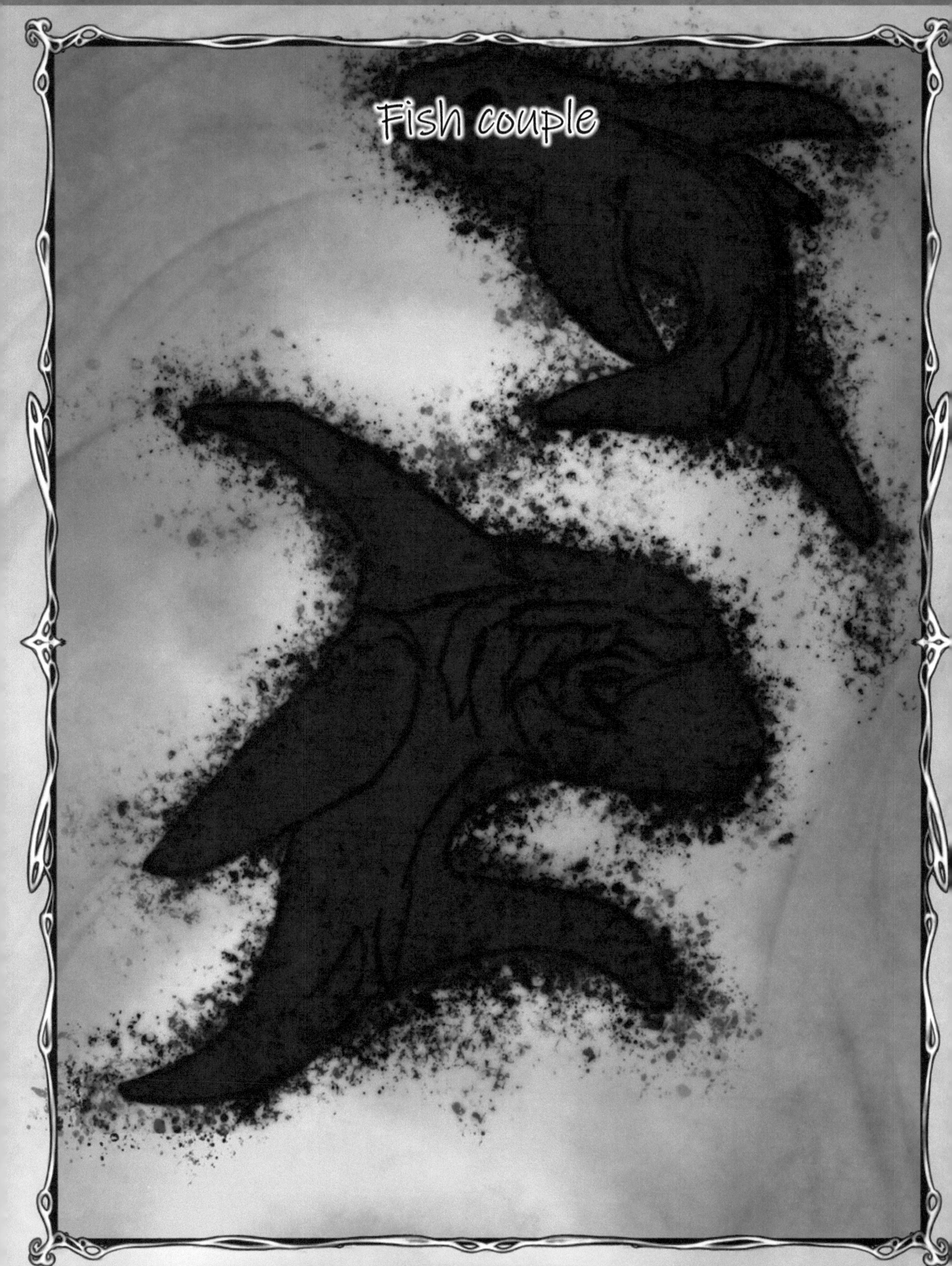

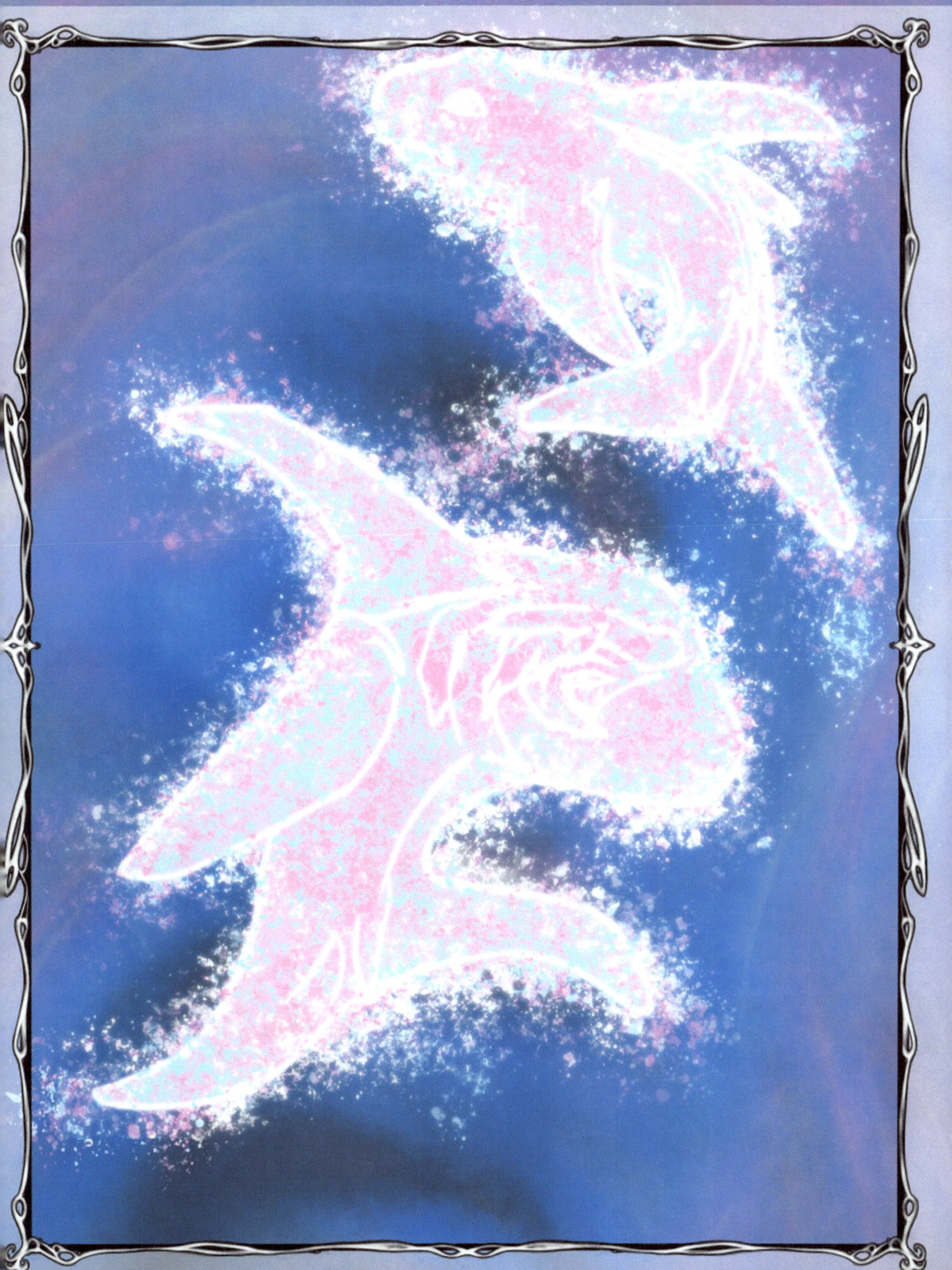

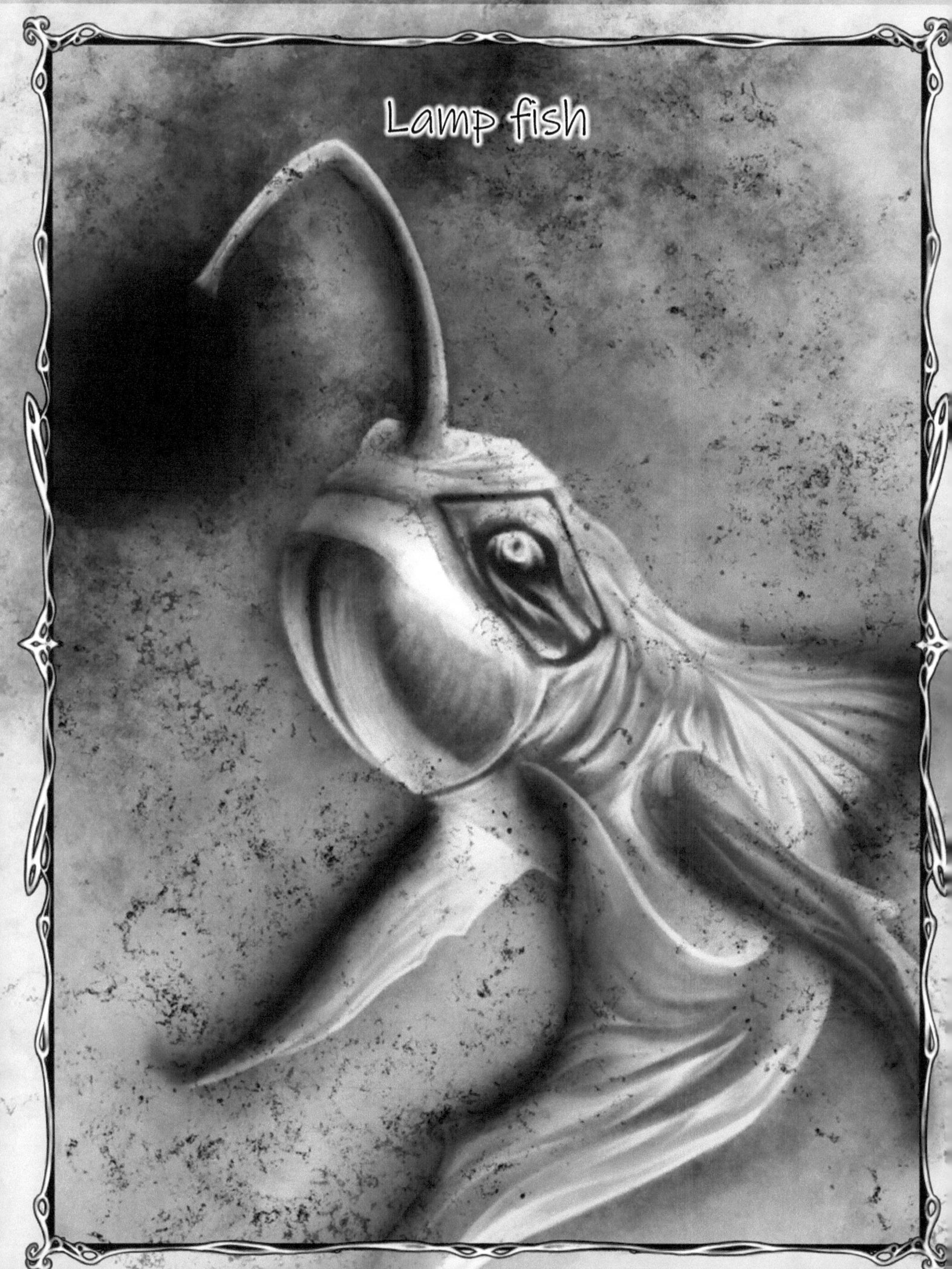

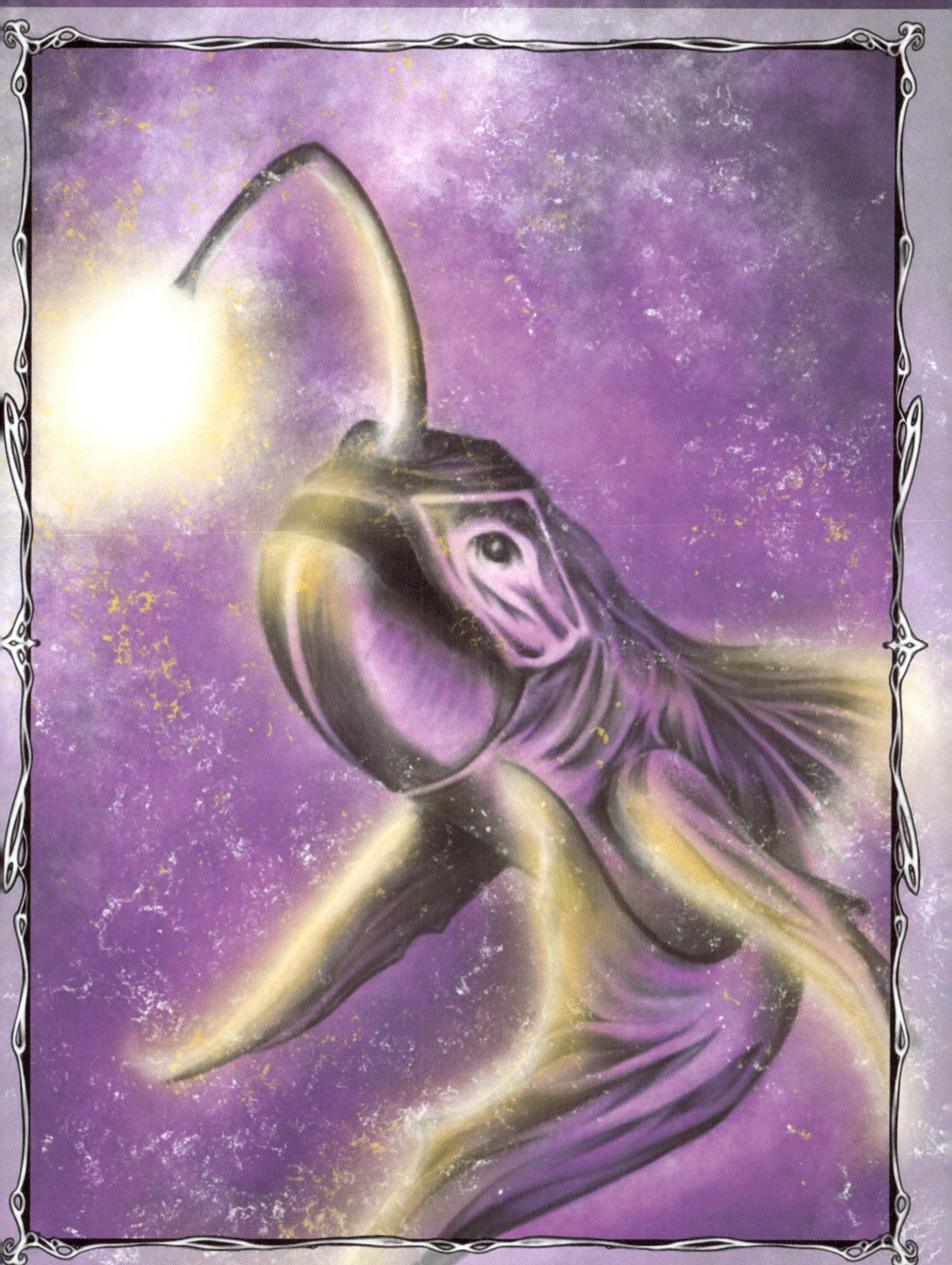

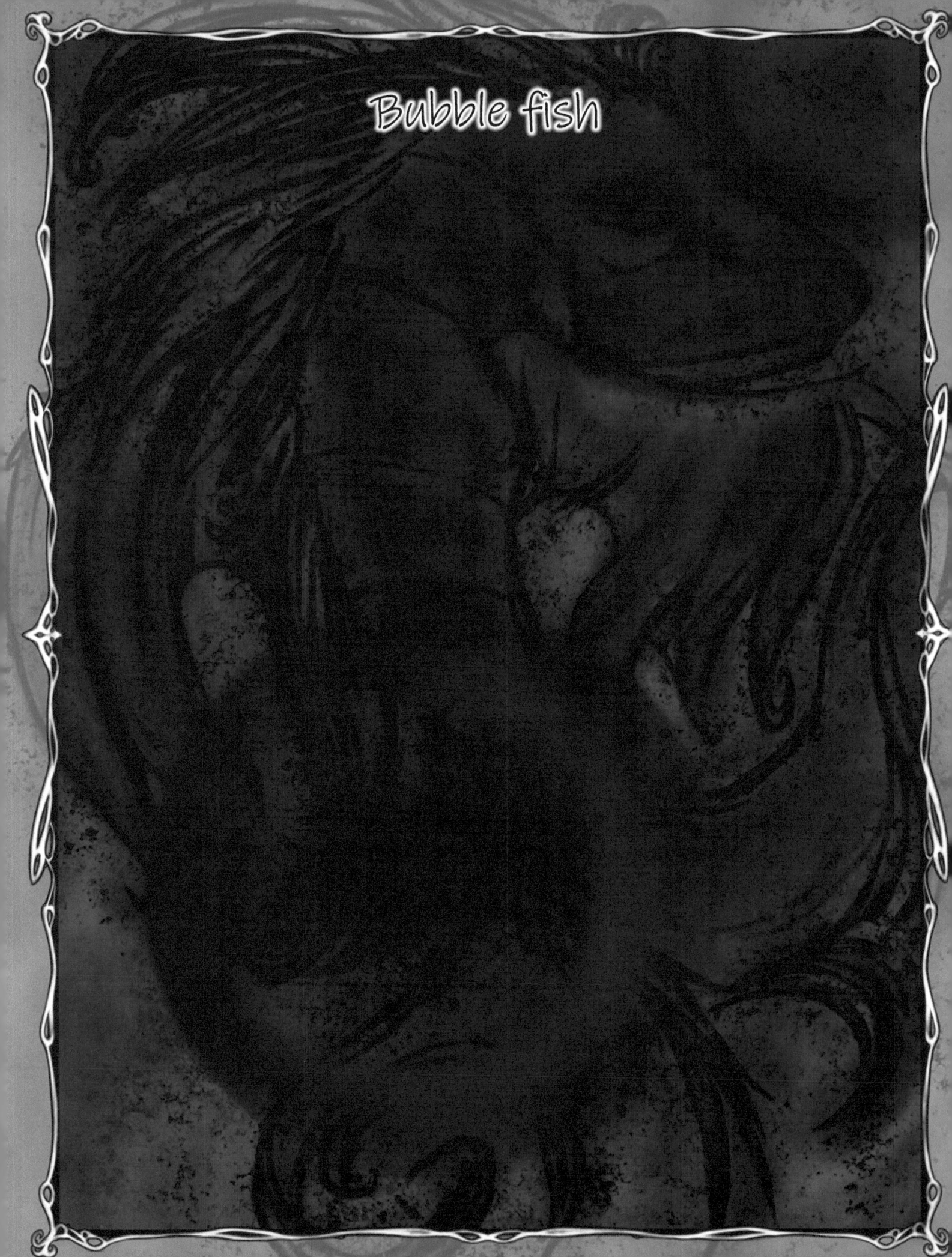
Bubble fish

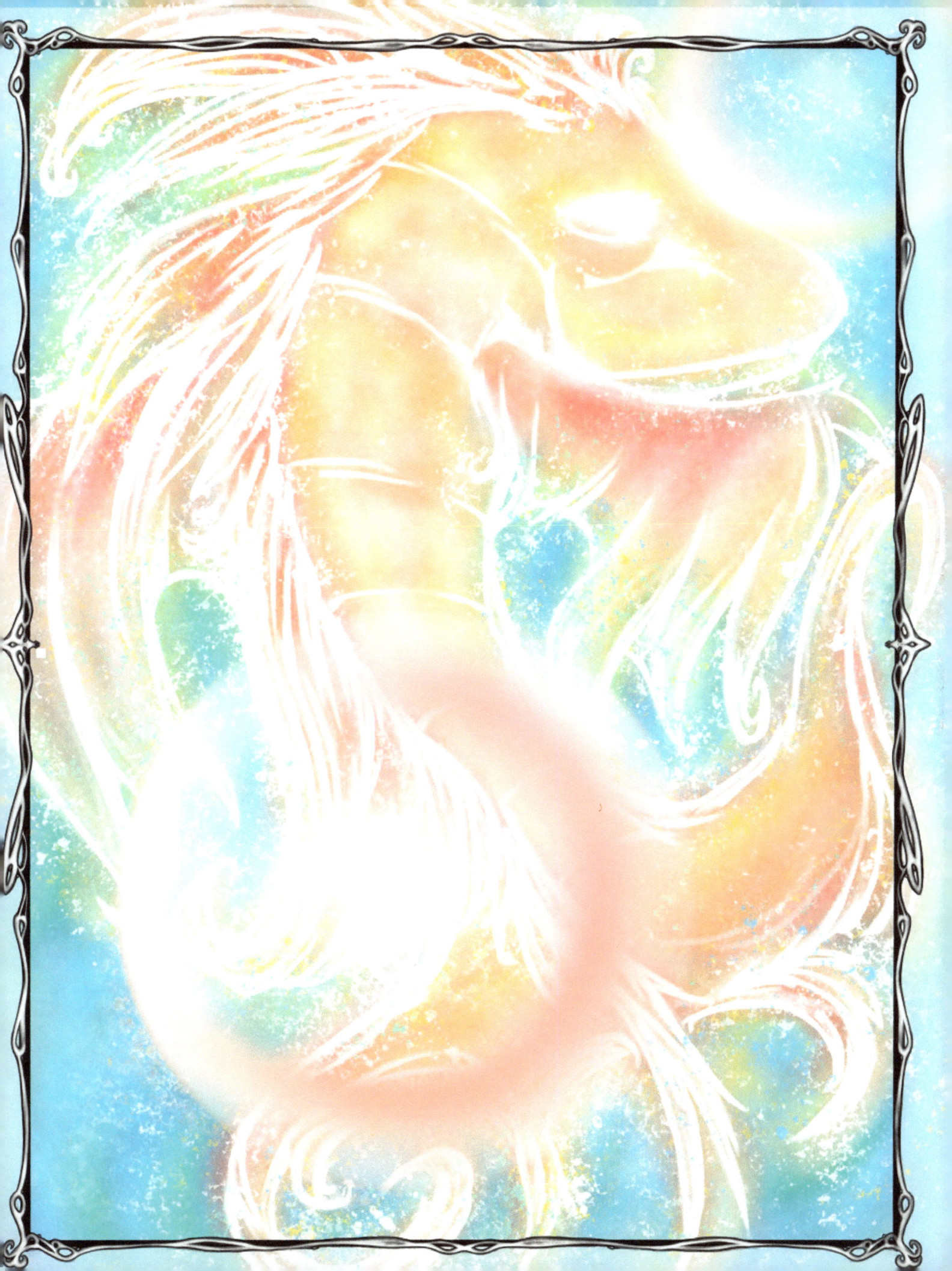

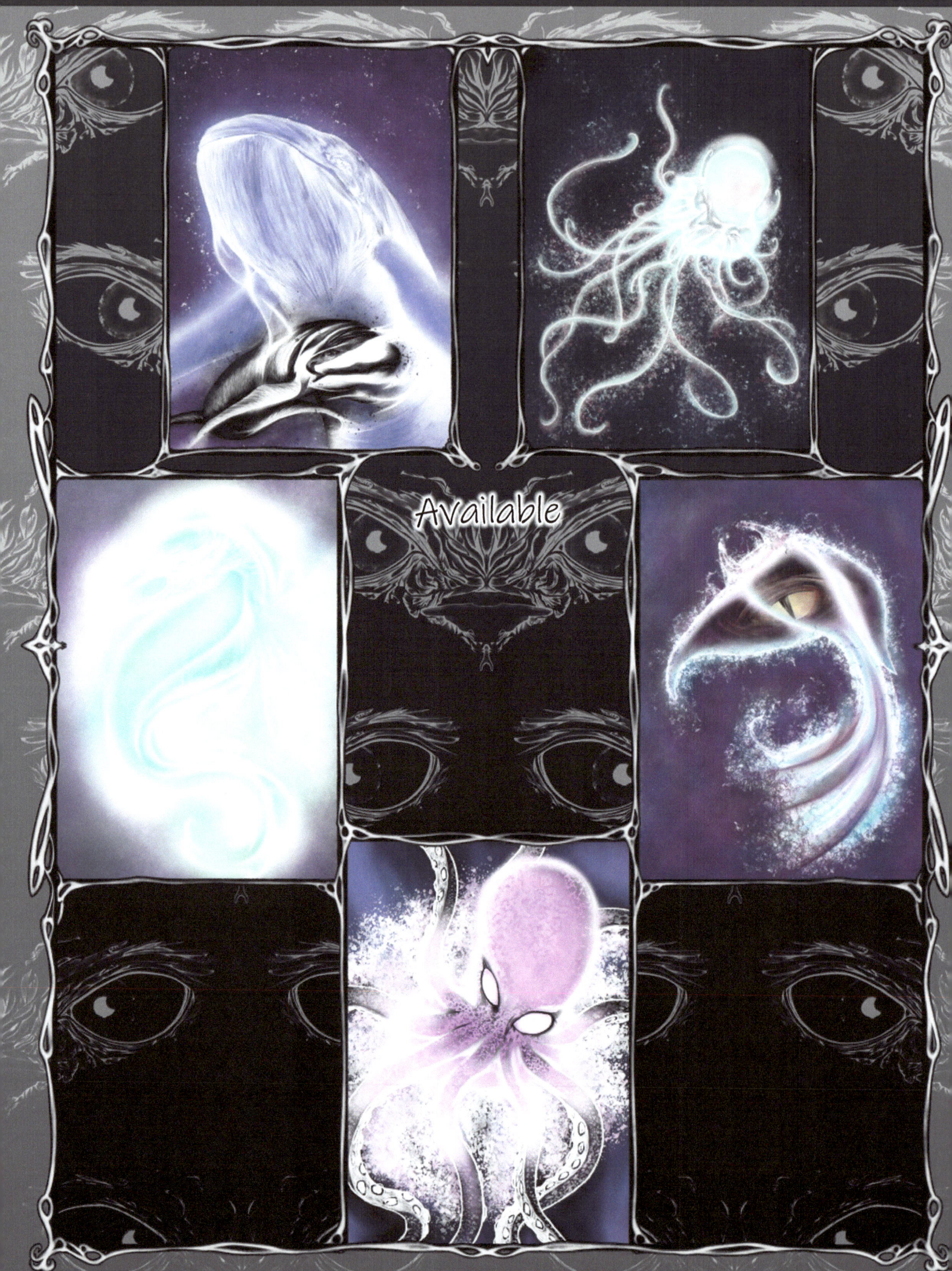

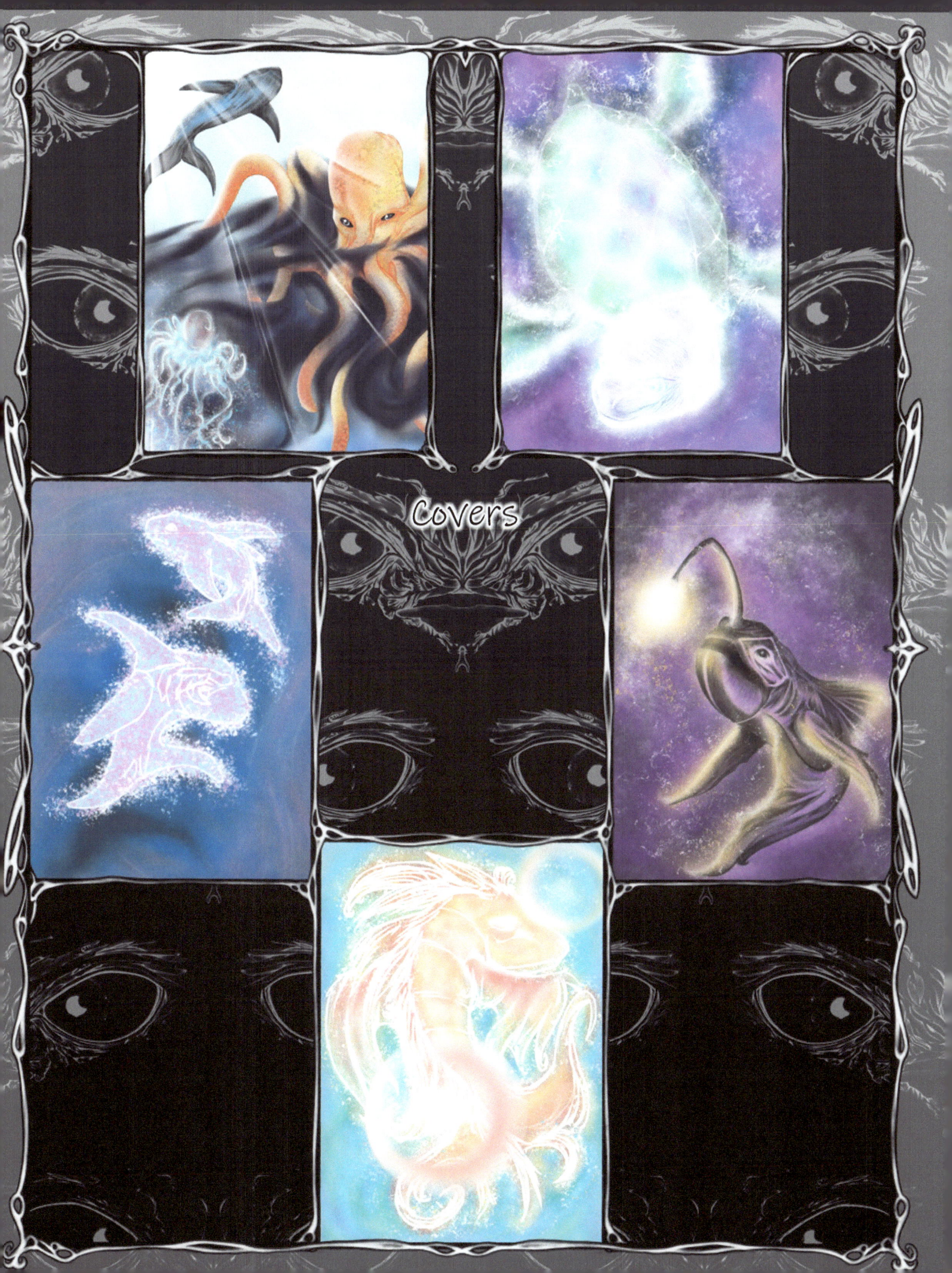

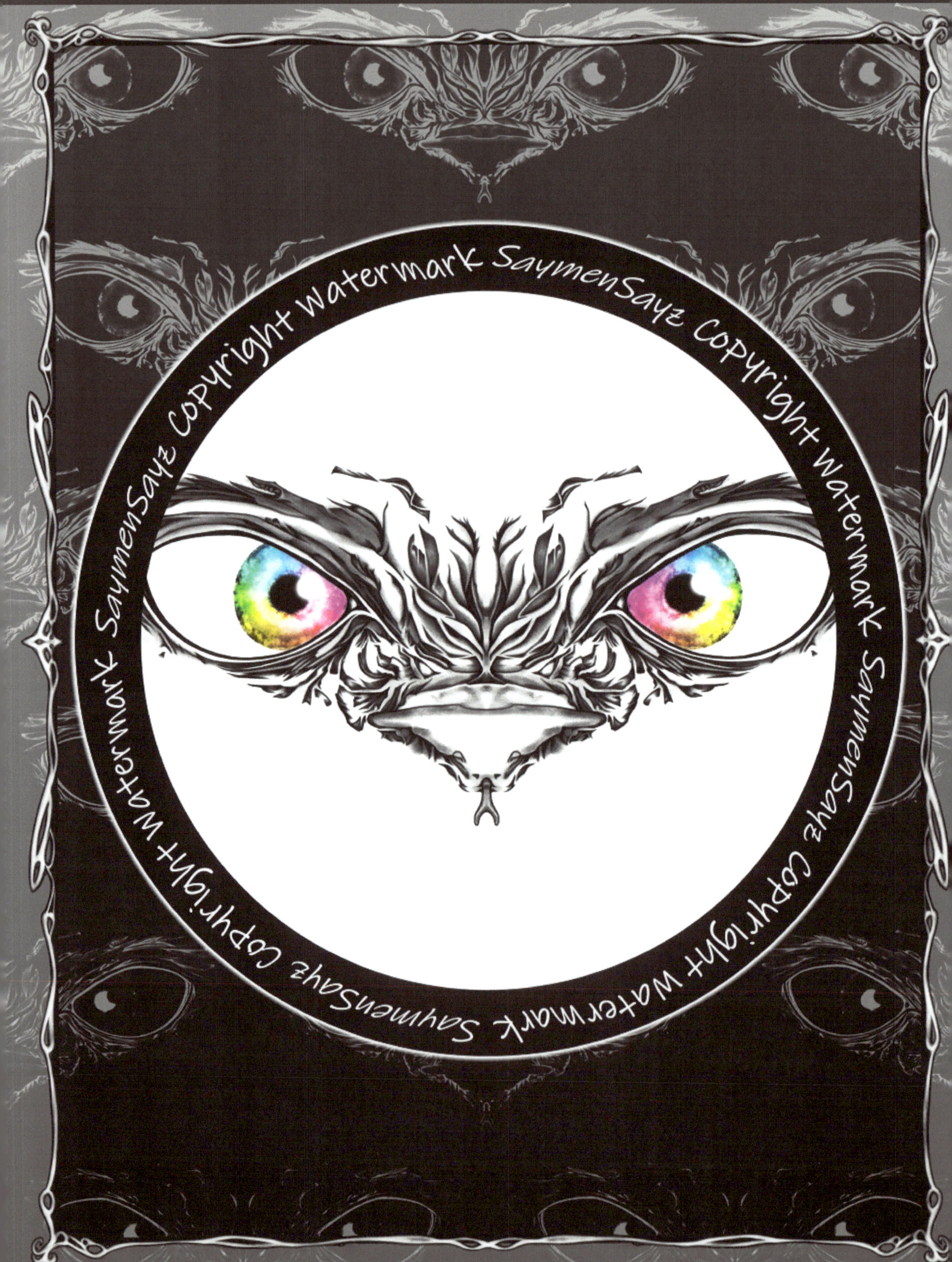

www.ingramcontent.com/pod-product-compliance
Lightning Source LLC
Chambersburg PA
CBHW051838210526
45473CB00005B/1928